EXISTENTIAL

QUESTIONS

BY JAX PAX

Table of Contents

Introduction

This book is very short but as it is a collection of contemplations there is value in reading it at least a few times. Keeping the book short allows the reader to revisit these contemplations without being intimidated by the task of reading a thick book. First time readers, may I recommend suspending judgement until the full book has been read? —It all weaves together. Second and third reads may be more effective than the first.

This book distils insights from years of my own thinking and from studying both ancient and modern philosophy on the topic of non-duality and the nature of consciousness, matter, growth and form. I have long been agitated by the views of some popular scientists—views which I would call one-mode-reductionism. Reductionism is useful but it can create serious problems when used in the wrong context or when the reductionist is unaware of the fact that he or she has reduced reality to a narrow part while ignoring the reality of the whole. Taken to its extreme, reductionism can form a worldview that leaves nothing recognizably beautiful nor worth caring for in sight.

Models and Reality

The physicist, Robert Shaw wrote, "You don't see something until you have the right metaphor to perceive it."

It seems to me that people form a mental model of the world that reduces themselves (or their brains) to machines or computers because that's all they have a concept of, without realizing they're thinking metaphorically. It can be useful to think in this way when engaged in reductionist forms of science, which are basically the ones that pay, but then they carry that thinking over to existential questions and dehumanize and torment themselves.

It seems to be in fashion that some philosophers, claiming to be promoting a so-called "spiritual" view, try to get around this with slightly more inspiring-sounding metaphors like the 'holographic-universe' model, but still, they don't seem to realize that what they're doing is using metaphor to create a mental model of reality rather than looking directly at reality.

Of all the machines humans have invented, the hologram does the best job of imitating reality, but it is still mechanistic and it's still not quite like reality itself.

So why form a model at all? In modern education, we are trained to practice reductionist thinking because it is useful in manipulating the natural world to bend it to our desires. It allows us to get a *grasp* of the world in some sense, but this way of thinking can trouble us when we are faced with existential questions.

"If anyone imagines he will get more by inner thoughts and sweet yearnings and a special grace of god than he could get beside the fire or with his flocks or in the stable, he is doing no more than trying to take god and wrap his head in a cloak and shove him under a bench. For whoever seeks god in some special Way, will gain the Way and lose god who is hidden in the Way. But whoever seeks god without any special Way, finds him as he really is… and he is life itself." Meister Eckhart

In Model-Dependent Realism, the claim is made that

reality should be interpreted based on scientific models of phenomena and that the only meaningful thing is the *usefulness* of the model. They claim that it is meaningless to talk of a "true-reality" as we can never be certain of anything.

I agree that we can never be completely certain of anything, but in some cases the model-ists, let's call them, carry that way of thinking over to matters that are beyond the realm of utility and persist in denying the importance of mystery and continue to affirm their simplified model of the world as if it represented the true-reality, forgetting that they had formed a simplified model for utility's sake to begin with.

There are many scientists who go beyond such a simple way of thinking, but the trouble is that many of the most well-known scientists are often the most reductionism-happy scientists, the model-ists, if you like. It is they who speak most confidently in support of the simplified world views that make for good commercial television and pop-science books that satisfy the low-bar required for mass market appeal.

Which brings us to the underlying theme of this book:

> *When you take the water out of the ocean, you take the ocean out of the water.*

What Comes First: Mind or Matter?

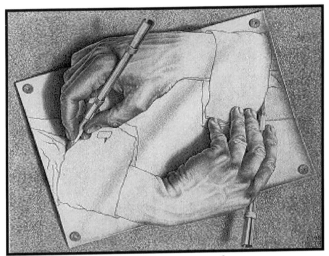

Escher's lithograph: Drawing Hands

Looking at Escher's famous lithograph of *Drawing Hands*—a hand drawing a hand drawing itself—a small child could marvel at that and wonder which hand drew which hand first.

But any adult can see that neither of those two hands drew the other—instead there was a third hand involved—Escher's hand drew the whole thing.

This sketch has a parallel in the question of—what comes first—mind or matter? We can examine the two endlessly and perhaps fail to see that neither one necessarily causes the other—they each move in unison and for all we know, there may be a third factor involved in the creation of reality, that paints the whole thing in.

This concept we learn from Escher is also relevant to the question of—What is a self? Or—If the self is an illusion, on whom is the trick played? To negate the self (as some do—thinking they are being cleverly spiritual) would be an error at the same low level of sophistication as it takes to assert the self as being isolated and not interdependent with the rest of the universe.

Examining the question closely we can determine that the self cannot be only the body, because it has attributes of the mind too. But it cannot be only the mind because it has attributes of the body also. The natural conclusion may be to assume that the self is the addition of body plus mind and to leave it there. But this can't be it either— body and mind move in unison and are never completely independent of one another.

Then we could attempt to go further by saying—the self is the possessor of the body-mind. But this too would be in error because there is no self that is completely independent of the body-mind.

So rather than being caught in this trap, as was the child trying to figure out which of Escher's hands came first, we can refer to Escher's teaching again and realize that the self may be another 'something' that is, for all we know, undefinable and beyond conception.

The root of the word 'define' is 'to bring to an end'. The mere definition of the word illuminates the fact that this mode of operation—attempting to reduce the self to a definition, or to a part, or to a collection of parts—is the wrong mode of operation for anyone who is wanting to cultivate a warm sense of spirituality to fall back on at times of existential struggle.

Why is There Something Rather than Nothing?

Can an actual nothingness even exist? I have seen a bowl of oranges and I have seen a bowl with no oranges, and I say there is 'nothing' in it. But that is only in relation to oranges. Of course, there was air in the empty bowl and space too, which is also something.

Our concept of 'nothingness' comes from our own relationship with the world in that when we see nothing that we are specifically looking for we say there is nothing. Or when we think about outer space, we imagine a void of solid objects and say there is nothing there. But space itself is something and so there is something there.

The whole concept of absolute nothingness may be complete nonsense for all we know. This also has relevance to the existential question—How did the universe begin? According to the Buddhist perspective on this—time is beginning-less. Next, we will look at time more closely.

What is Meant by Beginning-less Time?

"If the doors of perception were cleansed, every thing would appear to man as it is, Infinite. For man has closed himself up, till he sees all things thro' narrow chinks of his cavern." William Blake

The nature of time is more unusual than our immediate intuition suggests. This was revealed by physicists in the 20th century and demonstrated mathematically, but it can also be revealed by various thought experiments that were conceived of many centuries ago.

Consider a shooting arrow. If you were to examine the arrow's movement and could cut its movement up into time frames that were infinitely small, when could you observe that the arrow was moving? Never. If observed through a time frame that is infinitely small, the arrow appears to be stationary at every point. And so, it may be that there are only patterns and events, as opposed to 'time' as we know it in our coarse view of the world. The physicist Carlo Rovelli suggests this also as he writes:

"On closer inspection, in fact, even the things that are most 'thing-like' are nothing more than long events. [...] In the elementary grammar of the world, there is neither space nor time – only processes that transform physical quantities from one to another, from which it is possible to calculate probabilities and relations. At the most fundamental level that we currently know of, therefore, there is little that resembles time as we experience it."

And so, the ancient thought experiment on the moving-arrow begins to reveal the strange nature of time.

Now how about the speed of light in relation to our sense of time? When we look out at the stars we see those stars in the moment that we call "now". But since they are light-years away, the light we are seeing from the stars must have taken years to get here and therefore a star that is visible *now* might not even be there right now. It's mind-blowing to think of what this might mean if you reel it back to a shorter distance.

When I look at a tree just in front of me, I think of that as how the tree is 'now', but actually I am never quite seeing the tree as it is 'now'. I am seeing it slightly after it's time. Or to use a further analogy—when I hear a gun shot a split second after I see the smoke come out of the gun, it's obvious that I'm hearing a sound that is detached from its source. But because light travels so fast, it is much more difficult to break the association between the object and the sense of it when the sense of the object is visual. To some extent, our concept of time is caught up in our relationship with light.

To investigate the roots of our perception of time some more, we can look closely at the language we use regarding time. It's often the case that language distorts perception (or at least reveals a human form of perception), and this is also a factor in our perception of time.

Our perception of time is bound up with the use of spatial metaphors. So, let's first consider the spatial language we use. When I stand in front of a tree, I can look at it and say the tree is 'in space.' But saying the tree is '*in* space' implies that the tree somehow has an existence that is separate from space. Is space something that only *surrounds* things, or do we simply call that which surrounds things "space" because it is air-space that a solid object could move through? The tree is not 'in' space, it's what space is doing there. The universe is really all process. All happenings. Objects, are what we see when we cut the world up into separate parts based on their relationship to their utility to us as creatures. But space does not stop at the boundary of a solid object. It continues **as** the object. In a sense, the tree is what space is doing there. Space is tree-ing there.

A similar perspective can be taken using physics also. Combining Max Planck's equation (energy equals frequency multiplied by a constant) and combining it with Einstein's relativity equation (energy equals mass multiplied by the speed of light squared), we have energy is mass is frequency. Or in plainer English, energy is matter is movement. In a sense, everything we know to be the world—i.e. energy, matter and movement—flows as the one substance.

Just as it was an assumption of the coarse mind to see the tree as being 'in' space, it is also an assumption to see the tree as being 'in' time. Time is not necessarily spatial to begin with and so the concept of being 'in' time is really a metaphor borrowed from spatial thought. Useful, in our daily lives as we conceptualize time and go about the day, but not such an effective model when it comes to answering crucial existential questions.

Why Do We Come into This World?

The question—Why do we come into this world? —has in it the assumption that we did in fact 'come into' this world. But that would suggest that we came from elsewhere, as if a 'something' like us could somehow exist, just like this, without being immersed in a world, just like this.

But taking the human out of the world would be like taking the wave out of the ocean. Only in its interplay with—*and as*—the ocean, could it exist as a wave. If you attempt to remove the wave from the ocean, what you have is a bucket of water.

The philosopher, Alan Watts, wrote, "We do not "come into" this world; we come out of it, as leaves from a tree. As the ocean "waves," the universe "peoples.""

Watts paints a more beautiful and transcendent picture of our existence in this manner. If we are to believe that we "come into" this world, then we feel as if we don't belong. As if we are alien visitors, out of place, and far from home. Perhaps by no coincidence, that seems to describe just how people do feel when they are heavily entrenched in the cult of one-mode-reductionism.

The message from Alan Watts allows us not only to feel at home in the world but it simultaneously allows us to see our own uniqueness. It is both humbling and inspiring to fathom the reality that a growth on a placental wall eventually leads to a human being with a heart and her own unique character.

Is My Body a Spiritual Vessel?

"Language can become a screen which stands between the thinker and reality. This is the reason why true creativity often starts where language ends." Arthur Koestler

In conversations around spirituality—mostly new age spirituality—we often hear people make the statement, "My body is a spiritual vessel." This statement sounds enlightening on the surface but a closer look reveals it to be a flawed take on spiritual embodiment.

The flip-side to the view that the body is a spiritual vessel is that we then have the potential to feel trapped in the body when things are going badly. It is not necessary to see ourselves as ghosts in machines in order to have a spiritual view of life, and nor is it necessary if we want to be open to the possibility of an afterlife.

This point has been covered in various ways in the earlier essays on time, space, mind and matter, but let's approach the question from a new angle.

In this question, we can again see that language reveals the perception. In answering the previous question— "Why do we come into this world?"—we went from the notion that we 'come into' the world to Alan Watts' suggestion that we 'come out' of the world, which suggests that we are not visitors to this world but that we are 'of' this world. It's an improvement, but we can go one step further, as Alan Watts did while he elaborated his philosophy in, *The Book: On the Taboo Against Knowing Who You Are*. Rather than seeing ourselves as being 'of' the world, we can see ourselves 'as' the world.

To look more closely at the concept of a human being coming out of a placental wall or of a baby developing out of an embryo, let's consider what the well-known cognitive linguist and philosopher, George Lakoff, writes in his book, *Metaphors We Live By*:

"We conceptualize changes— […] from one state to another, having a new form and function—in terms of the metaphor, *The Object Comes Out of the Substance*."

George Lakoff is writing here of statements such as:

"I made a paper airplane 'out of' a sheet of paper." Or, "I made a statue 'out of' clay."

We are so in the habit of speaking this way that we take it for granted that it is perfectly true, all the while though, there is something being missed—in what way does the statue come 'out of' the clay? And in what way does the paper airplane come 'out of' the sheet of paper?

As George Lakoff demonstrates, we are working on the assumption that *the object comes out of the substance.* But surely the statue *is* the clay and the airplane *is* the paper. At the same time though, we can again see that the whole is not found in the parts. A paper airplane is not simply paper, and a statue is not simply clay. Matter cannot exist without form. There is no such thing as formless matter.

Now applying this to the thought of a human being

coming 'out of' the placenta or a baby being formed 'out of' an embryo, does that still make perfectly good sense?

We can go a little deeper, even still. There are more metaphors we live by that can illuminate something very interesting about how "things" appear.

Lakoff then mentions another metaphor that is relevant to this existential question regarding how things appear:

"Another way we can conceptualize making is by elaborating on direct manipulation, using another metaphor: *The Substance Goes Into the Object.*"

Examples of this metaphor, *The Substance Goes Into the Object*, include:

"She is turning 'into' a beautiful woman," or, "the water turned 'into' ice."

In this metaphor, it is assumed that—*the object is a container for the substance.* 'She' goes 'into'— 'a beautiful woman.' Looking more closely we can see how the metaphor creates a duality. The idea that the substance goes into the object, would suggest that the two are separate, yet neither the 'she' nor the 'beautiful woman' will ever be found separately on their own.

If we apply this realization to the concept of an embryo growing into a baby, we begin to see that a spatial metaphor has once again been borrowed from our confidence in spatial manipulation and has found its way into our world view. Is it true that an embryo grows 'into' a baby or that a baby grows 'out of' an embryo? I'd say we have revealed here that our intuitive conceptualization of growth and form is not accurately reflective of the true nature of reality. Rather than growing 'out of' or 'into' a baby, the growth somehow appears 'as' a baby when it is a baby.

At what point does something change from one thing to another? When is a seed no longer a seed but is instead a sprout? When is a sprout no longer a sprout but is a seedling? And when is a seedling no longer a seedling but is an adult plant? As we cannot have infinite words to describe each stage of growth, the answer must be— when you say so. In fact, it doesn't make sense even to say, "each stage", because even the stages themselves would be arbitrarily designated. Who decides the length of time for each stage, or the form of each stage?

Dōgen, a 13th century Japanese Buddhist philosopher known for his writing on the nature of time, speaks to this in his philosophy on 'Being-Time':

"We should not take the view that what is latterly ashes was formerly firewood. What we should understand is that, according to the doctrine of Buddhism, firewood stays at the position of firewood [...] There are former and later stages but these stages are clearly cut."

Buddhist philosopher, David Loy, elaborates in his book, Nonduality:

"[...] Firewood does not become ashes. There is the "being-time" of firewood, then the "being-time" of

ashes. If there are no non-temporal objects then the present does not gain its meaning or value by being related to the past or future: each event or being-time is complete in itself."

All this begins to raise questions as to the concept of 'making' all together. Is a tree 'made of' wood? Or is wood what you get when you cut the tree up? Isn't the tree existing *as* a tree-ness (or a that-ness) all the way through? Is there wood inside the tree? Or is there potential-for-wood in the tree?

So then, is a person 'made of' matter? Or is matter what you get when you deconstruct the person? To answer this, I will refer back to the earlier essay on Escher's *Drawing Hands*. Is a person 'made of' matter? The answer can either be yes, no, or neither yes nor no, depending on how you approach it. Surely, we will never find a person in the matter.

If we are not 'in' the world but instead we are 'as' the world, then we had it right as small children before the intellect became so clever as to get in the way, modelling a world-size map of the world and placing it over the world as if the intellect had to constantly put itself to use.

"The universe is not only stranger than we imagine, it is stranger than we can imagine." J.B.S Haldane

What Makes Me, Me?

When I was younger I used to wonder what would happen if I replaced a body part with a mechanical synthetic version? Would I still feel like myself? What if I continued to replace my body parts one by one, almost like a game of hangman played in reverse, until I was eventually all machine? First a leg. Then the other limbs. Then a kidney. Would I still be me? What if I kept going and replaced my stomach with an artificial version? And then a mechanical heart? Am I still me? What about this then—mechanical genitals? Then I really begin to wonder.

Is Everything Just Playing Out Like Clockwork?

A superficial understanding of science can lead to the assumption that the universe plays out like clockwork. As if the initial conditions were set up in the beginning, then someone hit the go button and everything since has followed in a predetermined manner. This again, is a mechanistic view. Those who make this assumption, without realizing it, are modelling the universe as a machine, as if there were nothing more to it than the straight forward Newtonian mechanisms of clockwork. They assume reality to be nothing but a cascade of atoms bumping into one another like a line of dominoes falling eternally in what could be called 'the billiard ball model' of reality.

Modern physics easily refutes this too, but again, the ancient philosophers had already done a good job. In this case it was the early Buddhists. The Buddhists approached this with a thought experiment that went something like this:

If the universe consists of tiny, indivisible particles, then the first question that comes to mind is—can two particles come into contact?

If we assume they can, then let's say the east side of one particle comes into contact with the west side of another particle. This suggests that the particles have an east and a west side, which means that they have parts, and therefore cannot be truly indivisible.

If we instead assume they do not have parts, then they must also have no size and so the particles could only contact one another by fusing together. But if the particles have no size, then if two particles can fuse, why not three particles? Or a thousand particles? Or the whole planet?

An objection could be to say that the particles do not need to come into contact in order to form matter. In which case, it is being assumed that there is a space existing between the particles. Since the particles are assumed to have no size, then what's to stop the whole universe from collapsing into one spot?

Through this thought experiment, the ancient Buddhists uncovered the truth—that the universe cannot be made up simply of tiny indivisible particles bumping into one another. There has to be something else going on. Something involving principles not visible in everyday reality. To assume that the universe simply plays out like clockwork would be an error.

Aren't We Just Monkeys?

Whether we humans are *more-than* monkeys may be a matter of personal opinion, but we can see that we are *different-from* monkeys in that we have qualities and faculties that monkeys do not have.

To say humans are the same as monkeys based on the fact that we can be classed as primates is like saying water is "just hydrogen" because it has a hydrogen part.

The qualities of water cannot be found in the qualities of hydrogen nor in the qualities of oxygen.

When you add the qualities of hydrogen to the qualities of oxygen, you would still not have the qualities of water.

The qualities of water are whole new qualities not found in its parts, nor in the sum of its parts.

Likewise, some of the qualities of a human being cannot be found in the parts of the human that came from earlier stages of evolution, and nor would you create a human being merely by adding those parts together. There is a unique whole that is human. To say we are 'monkeys' or that we are the same as other creatures who are also classified as 'primates' because we have evolved from them wouldn't be much more intelligent than saying we are 'nothing but fish' because we evolved from them too, only longer ago.

Reproduction is not replication. Even in just one generation, the offspring produced are noticeably different to their parents. This is why even many biologists these days use the term procreation rather than reproduction.

It is not that we are necessarily *better than* other primates, but we certainly are *different,* and in ways that we as human beings inevitably value. Our capacity to understand story. Our capacity to plan long term, to invent, and to create cultures. Probably our capacity to practice reductionism! And maybe even a heightened capacity for self-awareness and a greater ability at inhibition. Even if it were the case that some of these extra faculties can be troublesome and do more harm than good, they are still of value, if not only for the fact that they provide us with a meaningful opportunity to make long-term decisions for better or for worse. With great power comes great responsibility. And as the Holocaust survivor and author of Man's Search for Meaning, Viktor Frankl observed: life is made meaningful by a sense of responsibility.

How Can Purposeless Activity Be as Meaningful as Purposeful Activity?

In the psychological realm, something can be true and not true at the same time. Paradox seems to permeate the psychological realm in every corner.

People say, "I want my life to have a purpose," as if that were the only way for it to be meaningful. They are right and wrong at the same time.

Externally at least, it may be a good idea to pursue something that gives a sense of purpose but—if I do 'this' *because of* 'that' — then there is the implication that 'this' is not meaningful in itself. Therefore, purposeless action can be meaningful because it does not require a duality or a means to an end. The foundational philosophy of purposeless action suggests that 'this' is meaningful in itself.

Purposeless play shows its intelligence in even the most functional ways. The physicist, Richard Feynman, was stuck in a creative rut for a period of time before he changed his approach and began working on projects that appeared to have no utility or purpose at all. It was only while playing around with things curiously, that he was able to make discoveries that just so happened to be of immense utility. The ones that no one saw coming. The road to innovation often works on this principle.

Do We Have Free Will?

This question has stumped philosophers for millennia. In recent times, prominent philosophers have written about the subject as if believing in free will is pure superstition and as if not believing in free will is somehow more compassionate. They seem to have neglected the fact that if you rid the person of responsibility altogether, you also rid the person of a meaningful existence and perceive them, and the rest of the world, in mechanistic terms as if everything they ever do is pre-determined. It is a nihilist's dream.

What must first be addressed in answering this question is that the question itself is poorly defined. What is meant by free will? The power to make independent decisions and to act on them? The more you think about this, the more you realize how vague the idea is. But let's try to answer the question by asking—is there any possibility that an individual has any power at all to make conscious decisions, that are not illusory, to act or respond to stimuli in a particular way according to his or her own values? Whether or not we have *absolute* control over our actions is another question. But let's investigate whether a human being is simply living with the illusion of volition, or whether that is an extreme view, developed by those wanting an answer on a matter that is as yet not understood to the extent they might like to imagine.

I would first like to point out that the very same crowd who confidently push the idea that we do not have free will, are the very people who will also claim that consciousness evolved to begin with so that the creature can observe what is going on and make appropriate decisions. That seems to be forgotten in their rhetoric on free will.

Those who denounce free will altogether, like to point to Benjamin Libet's research on the matter, somehow neglecting the fact that even Libet himself did not think he had disproven free will.

The first experiments on free will were in 1964, when two German researchers placed a device over participants' heads to measure electrical signals while they performed a task. The participants were asked to flex a finger on the right hand repeatedly at any pace that pleased them, for up to 500 times per visit. This revealed a very subtle uptick in the electrical pattern which the researchers later called the readiness potential or Bereitschaftspotential. The researchers believed they had observed the brain readying itself to create a voluntary movement.

Twenty years later, Benjamin Libet made the case that not only was the brain readying itself for action, but that the brain makes its decision to act before the person is consciously aware of it. The idea spread like wildfire, as dramatic ideas do. And still to this day, even lay people bring it up in conversations as if it were written in stone that our brains decide what we will do and we are merely passive witnesses.

But Libet's original claim had rested on shaky ground to begin with, and studies in more recent years have made it all the more unlikely to be correct. Even Libet himself was less confident of the finding than those who like to promote the nihilistic perspective.

The original study was subject to numerous confounding factors. In the study, they had reported that the readiness potential fired at 500 milliseconds before the action and that the conscious decision was made only 150 milliseconds before the action. Thinking about this, it is hard to believe that the experiment ever developed authority in the science community. If the participant is reporting the timing of when they made the decision by looking at a clock and reporting the time, how could that possibly be accurate? Can you read a clock in a millisecond and commit the number to memory while also thinking about tapping your finger? Obviously not. The experimental method is very inaccurate.

Those confident claims against free will, seem all the more absurd when you realize that studies in more recent times have shown the Bereitschaftspotential may be something else entirely. There is no solid ground on which to assume it *causes* the action.

In 2012, Aaron Schurger and his colleagues at The National Institute of Health and Medical Research in Paris, found that the Bereitschaftspotential is actually a build-up of brain activity that happens while a person is assessing a situation. Since the participants in Libet's study were not given external stimuli to act on but were instead tapping the finger when they pleased, they would have been more likely to do so when the brain activity was at its peak as there was nothing else to base the choice on. It's a classic example of how isolating humans in a laboratory can sometimes lead to a poor understanding of how humans really are. *When you take the wave out of the ocean, you take the ocean out of the wave.* Had they been able to study humans in a more dynamic situation, they may well have observed volition. Although I doubt they would have, because the map would inevitably have been mistaken for the territory while using reductionist methodology.

The legacy of the Bereitschaftspotential gets even less impressive when you find other studies have revealed it to be simply a symmetry-breaking signal. When monkeys were studied with the task of choosing between two equal options, a separate team of researchers observed that the Bereitschaftspotential correlated with the monkey's upcoming choice before the monkeys were even presented with the options. Or in other words, what was previously thought to be brain activity that causes action, is actually brain activity that occurs regardless.

In 2012, Schurger and his colleagues decided to repeat Libet's experiment and to avoid unintentionally cherry-picking brain noise, they included a control condition in which people didn't move at all. Using artificial intelligence, they were able to find the brain activity correlating with the finger tapping. It was found to be at about 150 milliseconds—the same time as the participants had reported making the decision. So, in other words, the interpretation of the Libet study had created a whole lot of drama over nothing. People's subjective experience of having made a decision to act does coincide with the action.

Of course, these less dramatic findings never made headlines. News travels fast only when it shocks and disturbs.

The more recent findings may be wrong too, and they don't tell us much about how this really works. But what's important to point out is that the mystery is still there. It's important not to be too quick to believe a confident one-mode-reductionist when they make such a lofty claim as to say we do not have free will. Our sense of volition is essential to our sense of responsibility and to our sense of meaningfulness. It is known by clinicians that this is an essential factor in mental health and so I find it alarming that certain writers have made such confident claims against free will without having done thorough research into the matter.

"Given the issue is so fundamentally important to our view of who we are, a claim that our free will is illusory should be based on fairly direct evidence... Such evidence is not available." Benjamin Libet (2004)

What is the Meaning of Life?

When a question is as long-standing as—What is the Meaning of Life? —we should be suspicious that the question itself is being asked in the wrong way.

Looking at the question with fresh eyes it becomes obvious that the question itself is worded very poorly in a linguistic sense. What does the question even mean? It will be much easier to get to the heart of the matter if we re-word the question to unearth what is really being asked.

What is really being asked is not—What is the meaning of life?, but—Is *my* life *significant*? If the answer to this question is not immediately obvious, as is the case for many, then the questioner can benefit from a simple thought experiment that is often practiced in meditation.

Begin by considering the life of a baby, any baby, and ask this question of their life. Is the baby's life significant? Of course, the answer is yes. Who would have any doubt? Now imagine that baby has aged, she is 2 years old, 3 years old, 4, 5 etc. And ask the question again at each point along the way. Is there ever a point where the child's life becomes insignificant? Again, it is clear that there is never a point when the child's life suddenly becomes insignificant. But then we get to puberty and the person, who was formerly a child, may no longer be endearing to some. Many of us begin to judge one another from puberty onward based on a measure of utility. But still, it would be extremely cruel to say the person's life was not significant.

Now repeat the thought experiment with a person in mind who you find most easy to appreciate. After thinking that through you will begin to see that the core significance of a human being is not within the realm of measure.

Once this realization has been made, it may be clear to see that measuring the core worth of oneself would also be in error. We don't judge a sausage dog's life to be insignificant because it's useless. In fact, people spend a lot of money on sausage dogs purely because they appreciate their presence. It is the same with a baby. And we do not judge a disabled person's life to be insignificant because they are not of utility. In fact, if the caretaker is interested in spiritual learning, it could be argued that the disabled person is doing as much for the caretaker as the caretaker is doing for the disabled person.

But this doesn't completely solve the original question — Is my life significant? The question begs an answer not only to — do I have a right to exist, but also to the question—why must I suffer?

Well the surest answer to that is to point out that—just as a three-year-old cannot fathom the mind of a thirty-year-old—perhaps no human being can fathom the mind of god (or the intelligence of the cosmos—if you prefer).

Anybody with a good deal of intelligence themselves can accept that there is likely to be some kind of intelligence about the universe that is beyond the scope of human understanding. Why assume, with certainty, that that intelligence would be nothing but a hard, cold, calculating intelligence that could not possibly possess any sense of justice at all, when we ourselves are a part of this universe and have a sense of justice?

The Nobel prize-winning physicist, Sir Roger Penrose, wrote in his book, *The Emperor's New Mind*, that computers cannot possibly compute a sense of meaning because in order to do so they'd have to take one instruction for why a thing is meaningful, then another to explain what is meant by meaningful, and yet another to explain what is meant by that and so on ad infinitum. Us human beings though—we have a *sense* of meaning lingering in the background activity of our awareness. And a *sense* of justice too.

In modern life, we are easily led to believe that the intellect can solve any dilemma. But the intellect is really quite a narrow part of experience and it does not encompass our whole capacity as human beings. As mentioned earlier, the root of the word 'define' is 'to bring to an end.' And so, we should not be surprised when attempts to *define* meaning, life, or soul, take us to a spiritual desert, a dead end, a lifeless view of the world and of ourselves that has drawn the human out of the human and reduced the being to a collection of parts, which each on their own are mechanistic and without soul.

But the whole cannot be found in the parts. The properties of water cannot be found in the properties of hydrogen, nor in the properties of oxygen, nor in the sum of the two. And likewise, the warm spirit of a being cannot be found in any part of her, nor in any description of her, nor in any argument as to *why* she should exist. Her worth cannot be measured yet it can so easily be sensed.

A common argument against the meaning of life is that the intellect and memories and even the maturity of character can seem to slide away from a person when they acquire Alzheimer's Disease or Dementia. But then there is the possibility that, just as the music coming from a radio isn't really coming from a radio but is actually coming from a transmission tower, memories may also be stored non-locally and the brain may simply be a marker or a receiver. Even the self-acclaimed militant atheist, Richard Dawkins, recently admitted in an interview that he likes to consider the idea that maybe memories are stored non-locally like the information stored in the iCloud. This is simply an example, that uses a mechanism we are familiar with as a potential metaphor. The true nature of consciousness would likely be entirely different and resembling something (if anything) that we do not currently understand. Or perhaps that's just it— consciousness may not *resemble* anything at all. It may only be us humans who look to understand consciousness by seeking resemblance to something simple and mechanistic.

It may be that neuroscientists are mistaking the map for the territory. After all, if the brain, and consciousness, worked in as straightforward a manner as some (but certainly not all) well-known neuroscientists suggest, then why wouldn't we be seeing 100% correlations in neuroscience studies rather than the much lower correlations that are actually seen?

There's an old story about a debate between a priest and a philosopher. The philosopher suggested that the last barrier to "god" was the concept of god. As the priest was shocked the philosopher elaborated, "The horse that you mount and that you use to travel to a house is not the means by which you enter the house. You use the concept to get there, then you dismount and go beyond it." The heart of mysticism lies in knowing beyond knowledge.

"Men are afraid to forget their minds, fearing to fall through the Void with nothing to stay their fall. They do not know that the Void is not really void, but the realm of the real dharma." Huang Po

"It is too clear, and so it is hard to see— A dunce once searched for a fire with a lighted lantern. Had he known what fire was, he could have cooked his rice much sooner." Mumon

"It is as atheistic to affirm the existence of God as to deny it. God is being itself, not a *being." Paul Tillich*

Recommended Reading and Viewing (with a similar message)

- *The Book: On the Taboo Against Knowing Who You Are* by Alan Watts
- *Challenging the Nihilists on Free Will with Aaron Schurger* on the Jax Pax Channel (a podcast on YouTube and most other podcast platforms)
- *Models and Reality: A conversation between Dr Iain McGilchrist and Jax Pax* on the Jax Pax Channel (a podcast on YouTube and most other podcast platforms)
- *The Matter with Things* by Dr Iain McGilchrist
- *The Master and His Emissary* by Dr Iain McGilchrist
- *Nonduality* by David Loy
- *Interdependence and Reality: Geshe Tenzin Namdak and Rupert Sheldrake* Podcast on Rupert Sheldrake YoutTube channel
- *Wholeness and Implicate Order* by David Bohm
- *Introduction to Emptiness* by Guy Newland
- *The Cloud of Unknowing* by Anonymous Author

(an ancient classic)

- *Awareness* by Anthony de Mello
- *Metaphors We Live By* by George Lakoff
- *The Other Shore* by Thich Nhat Hanh

Previously by Jax Pax

- The Artist's State of Mind: A Guide to Accessing the Flow State Through Mastery of Your Chosen Craft
- How Yoga Really Works

This topic has been discussed on the **Jax Pax Channel podcast**, most specifically with Dr Iain McGilchrist on the episode titled Models and Reality. The Jax Pax Channel podcast can be accessed via YouTube and most other podcast platforms.

To follow Jax Pax on Instagram: @jaxpaxworx

Blog: www.jaxpax.substack.com

Counterintuitivethought@gmail.com

Extracts from The Artist's State of Mind

Anger and Frustration

"Research finds that anger management therapies- like hitting pillows or other attempts at "catharsis" or "getting it all out" - increase rage, rather than decrease it [...] Expression isn't always necessary, contrary to popular belief."[1]

—Bruce Perry, M.D., PH.D., author of 'Born for Love'

Since frustration (or anger) is encountered so often on the road to mastery, a deep understanding of the nature and meaning of frustration is essential in the pursuit of mastery. But when we talk about anger or frustration, how do we know we are each talking about the same inner experience? An outward display of aggression is not always accompanied by the inner experience of anger. When attacking the ball during sport for example, the inner sensation may be completely different to that uncomfortable feeling that we experience when we're in the heat of an argument. And acts of "passive aggression" do not really involve any outward display of aggression at all, but we can infer that the person is experiencing anger internally when being passive aggressive.

An outward display of aggression is sometimes warranted and can be an effective action, but when it *is* the most suitable action, I am suggesting that it never carries with it the internal discomfort of what we can call "anger". The English language is very under-equipped when it comes to describing emotions. In some languages, such as the Tibetan language, there are hundreds of words for describing emotions and they each have very distinct meanings.

Before I describe my own view on anger, I would like to point out that I believe compassionately motivated aggression is actually one of the most *under*-employed actions of all in everyday life. In short — in this culture at least — we are generally too polite towards people when they are acting destructively and there are many serious consequences of that. But the anger I am referring to is something else. I see it, as the Tibetans do, as being indicative of a deluded perception.

We use the one word, *anger*, to describe both situations (the destructive form of aggression and the compassionate form of aggression) but this is only because the English language does not equip us to decipher between the two in our speech. This lack of expression in our language then leads to a lack in our emotional awareness because we switch off to the difference in sensation between the two emotions. Most people, in western cultures, are not aware that there even is a difference in internal sensation between compassionately motivated aggression and that anger that is indicative of a distorted perception. It never occurs to them to take notice of it. The Tibetan language, on the other hand, is more well-equipped for describing emotions because the Tibetan culture has grown around Buddhism and its meditation practices. Because of this, there have been enough people in Tibetan culture who were aware of the subtle differences in emotional sensations that they were able to talk about those differences with each other and to see the need to have unique words to decipher between the array of emotions.

In Tibetan, the compassionately motivated anger is called *khongtro* while the word *shyédang* refers to hateful anger.

My own definition for anger is:

'Anger (or frustration) is the discomfort that arises when an urgent message from the unconscious mind is being blocked from consciousness. Anger is there to motivate us to search for an alternative idea or perception, not to motivate us to act in anger.'

Pain is not necessarily "bad" in itself. Without pain, you could not keep your body out of danger. When you touch a hot stove, pain lets you know to move your hand away before you are seriously burnt. Negative emotions are painful for the same reason. They motivate us to take action or change our perception.

It seems to me that anger has been misunderstood as if it is meant to prompt the individual to attack. Actually, anger is not intended to motivate us to attack. Anger is there to draw attention to the deluded, or ineffective perception that we are holding on to. It is uncomfortable for the sake of motivating us to *change* our perception–not for the sake of motivating us to carry on as we are. If it were intended to motivate us to act upon the perception that is already there, then surely it would feel pleasurable. It isn't the anger that is bursting to get out; it's the alternative perception that is bursting to get out.

Have you ever tried to solve a problem and become intensely frustrated only to find after hours of wasted time that you could have fixed the problem much more easily if you had only noticed a different way of doing so? And as soon as that new idea was let through to your conscious mind, the feeling of frustration disappeared, am I right? Because that sensation of frustration was the unconscious mind tapping at your door saying, "I have a message for you". Once you had listened to that sensation and let go of the constraints that your perspective was hammered between, only then was it possible for the message to be brought into awareness. So, contrary to popular belief, forcing through a task in anger does not necessarily aid in overcoming an obstacle.

Really, anger (or frustration) is meant to be useful, but not in the way it is most commonly used. It is meant as a marker rather than a motivator. Anger needs to be uncomfortable if that's what it takes to grab our attention. Anger is brought about by an ineffective view of — or approach to — the situation at hand.

Pigeon-Holing

*"I do not believe in styles anymore. [...] When you have
no style, you say, ok here I am as a human being, now
how can I express myself totally and completely? That
way you will create a style [your own] as a process of
continuing growth."*
—Bruce Lee

In artistry, it can be very limiting and ineffective to bow
to the categories that have been set in place through
evolving traditions. When the artist places herself in a
pigeon-hole, that comes with both advantages and
disadvantages. For example, an aspiring songwriter might
stick to the category of country music. This makes the
whole pursuit of musicianship so much easier to navigate
than it would be without a clear genre to conform to as
she knows exactly what skills she needs to learn and how
and where to get them. She will also know where to
market herself and who to network with, and will
practically have a template for the whole pursuit. But
fitting into a category like this comes with its drawbacks

too. In some respect, that country songwriter's creativity will be limited by the constraints of what can be thought of as country music. An alternative approach is to loosen up the category and open up to influence from other genres. By detaching from the label of "country musician", her creative options are freed up. She can then choose the boundaries of her artistry consciously and add elements of other genres as they inspire her.

So, to categorize oneself — which is often an unconscious action — is potentially very limiting. Maybe we do need to think and move within categories at times in order to ease progress, but it's important to be aware of this tendency to categorize and to question whether it really is for the best or whether the categories just appear to be convenient on the surface.

Sophistication

It is said of olives that they are an acquired taste. You won't find many children who love eating olives. They much prefer something sweet. Like grapes. And it's just as well, because olives are bitter and a bitter taste potentially signifies poison in the natural world. For this reason, we are instinctively suspicious of bitter foods when we first encounter them, but with long term exposure to them we can sometimes become unusually partial to them. Even addicted to them. Especially when they are artificially laden with sugar too.

Wine is an example of a bitter food that takes time to develop a taste for. Hence its association with sophistication. When you want to be in a different class to the unsophisticated people—namely, children—it helps to demonstrate that you have a taste for something that no unsophisticated person (child) would take interest in. Hence the practice of wine and cocktail drinking at the high end of town (especially when served with olives).

But sophistication is not only relevant at the high end of town. The other end of town has its own brand of sophistication. Customary displays of sophistication observed at cocktails parties are forms of *overt prestige* while its counterparts observed in dirty pubs are forms of *covert prestige*. Rum is, to the man at the pub, what wine is to the woman at the cocktail party.

In the world of music, sophistication works in much the same way. It is those forms of music that have an acquired taste, such as acid jazz, that we consider to be "sophisticated". It may be no coincidence that its name, *acid* jazz, gives away hints of resemblance to bitterness.

Sophistication is not a full bunk-worthy concept however. There are genuine advantages to sophistication. Many art-forms that are considered to be sophisticated are genuinely valuable. After all, there is a quality to acid jazz that other forms of music can't offer and I'm sure its enthusiasts can verify the value in its qualities and in the culture surrounding it. But sophistication on its own does not *necessarily* signify *better* art. The question really comes back to what is being communicated. For example, if you want to communicate something universal about human relationships to the masses, then a popular style of singer-songwriting may be the best art form. But if you want to experience a more subtle and unusual feeling, maybe more advanced technical skills and a sophisticated art form like jazz will do the job.

The Past

"The image of the thing is not the thing." – Jiddu Krishnamurti

In an artist's lifetime, there are times when she feels she has hit that sweet spot we call being in the zone. It is different to simply going through the motions of playing the song. When the song is played with full sincerity, when the musician *is* the song, the performance is experienced with a quality to it, a realness, that is sensed by the performer as well as by the audience.

Once an artist has felt such an experience there is a tendency to want to repeat it. The musician may think to herself, "I wish I could play it again like I played that day", but, as many artists report, the attempt to repeat the experience *as it was*, always fails. It fails because the want to repeat the experience is not the same as *being* the experience. Or in other words, the memory of the experience is not the *actual* experience. The image of the thing is not the actual thing. The state she was in at that moment when she hit the sweet spot was not a state of wanting to repeat something of the past. She just did it. She *was* the song. Songs say something. She was saying something. That was her approach at the time. Not, "I will perform the song like I did it the other time", but instead, just communicating the song. Being it. Playing it. Enjoying it. Dancing it through.

Instruction

Playing video games can be a surprisingly effective learning experience. When you play a video game with enough skill and focus at some point you may lose yourself in flow. At that moment, you are not thinking in terms of instruction. You are just doing what you are doing. You forget that you are there in front of a screen.

But most of the time when we are going about activities we do not act in this way. We distrust our abilities. We assume that even the simplest tasks require a monotonous level of control. Giving ourselves instructions as if we have split ourselves in two. As if we were there with the game controller, as one self, directing the lesser self. Apparently, there are two of me, and the other half of me doesn't know jack about anything—he needs my instructions for his every move. I push him around all day as if he doesn't know what I know. He is the incompetent one. I know best. All the while, I am neglecting the fact that there is actually only one of me.

There is no part of me that is separate to me. So why can't I just trust it? Why can't I just play everything I do, as if I'm in that video game mode where I'm lost in flow? Why can't I drive my car like that instead of dividing me up as if superior me needs to keep an eye on subordinate me? Can I *be* the whole action rather than looming over myself?

Social Authority

In the pursuit of mastery, we can be led astray by the distortion of our perceptions that social authority creates. There is a common strategy in marketing called *social proofing*. Social proofing occurs when the display of attitudes of higher- or equal-status group members influence an individual's perception. Social proofing can be induced intentionally, for example when a commercial shows attractive people enjoying and worshipping the product being sold. But it can also happen indirectly. An example of this is when a person hears a song on the radio — if they don't know anything about the song they might think it's nothing special. But then they hear that same song in a movie and in a shopping center and at a party, and they hear it was ranked highly on *Rolling Stone*'s Greatest Songs of All Time list. The more they encounter the song in this way, the more social proofing they are receiving regarding the song, and so its prestige is building. After hearing the song in this variety of contexts, the song may begin to appear to be ingenious. For an artist who wants to create work of genuine value, it can be a disaster to fall for social proofing like this. Searching for the qualities in the song that led to its great success might only lead the artist astray because it wasn't necessarily the artwork itself that made the song popular. The song may have risen to that level of popularity by means of social proofing. By worshipping and replicating what is really just a social fad, the artist will waste time creating work that has no value in tomorrow's culture.

A similar situation to the one described above is what I like to call "the vintage effect". That is, the tendency for older works to be valued more highly than recent works. It is often said that music was better in the past than it is today. But those statements are neglecting the vintage effect. When an artwork has aged, it has built up in it a lot of history, social authority and nostalgia. It has stood the test of time, and to some extent, that is impressive in itself. But the idea that older music was better is an illusion, created mostly in this way. (As a side note: the perception that old music was better also comes partly because "old music" encompasses the best songs out of half a century of music while "new music" usually only refers to the past five years at most).

Excessive submission to social authority is one of the biggest killers of innovation. Things that carry social authority can only ever be things that already exist as being popular and accepted. A good way to side-step the hypnotic cage that social authority traps us in is to explore areas that are not considered to be prestigious or valid. The most innovative of the popular musicians are always influenced partly by music genres that are unpopular. By finding the best aspects of those less popular genres and bringing them into play with the qualities of a more popular style of music, they are able to create a fresh sound that a mainstream audience is ready for.

Even in sports, bowing to social authority can stunt performance. The American high jumper Dick Fosbury was laughed at when he began jumping over the bar in such an awkward way. Nowadays, the "Fosbury flop" is the standard method in high jump.

The key to avoiding the rut of submission to social authority is to bring the focus back to creating true value. Rather than trying to *be something*, why not aim to *do something*. If you're making music, your aim is most likely to communicate something to the listener. If you're playing tennis, you want to win beautifully. If you're designing a house, your aim might be to design a house that creates a good vibe. By focusing on the task at hand without needing to impress or to blindly fit in, the constraints of social authority are lifted and innovation is made possible.

Submission to social authority doesn't just hinder innovation; it also stands in the way of enjoyment. The flow state is a rare occurrence for people who believe they need social authority to instruct their every move.[2] Some people only seem to appreciate sights and experiences that are accepted as being valid and glamorous, like seeing the Eiffel Tower, for example. But these experiences are not necessarily any better than the happenings that we are fortunate enough to witness on an ordinary day. Many things can be seen as being more miraculous and entertaining than famous monuments and landmarks if we take off the distorting lens of social authority.

Aversion to Solitude

"The fear of rejection when one wants acceptance can cripple initiative and negate personal autonomy."[3]
—Psychologist, Philip Zimbardo, creator of the famous Stanford Prison Experiment

"All of humanity's problems stem from man's inability to sit quietly in a room alone."
—Blaise Pascal

"In technological societies, we spend about one third of the day alone, a much greater proportion than in most tribal societies, where being alone is often considered to be very dangerous."[4]
—Mihaly Csikszentmihalyi

A person who strongly dislikes being alone will have difficulty in developing one of the most important character attributes of an innovator — the potential to employ initiative. The pursuit of mastery will inevitably involve periods spent in solitude while thinking, reading, and practicing, as skills and understanding are developed and deepened. Fear of solitude is one of the strongest fears across all people, though it does not affect everyone. And for most people, it can be quickly reduced through a better understanding of the nature of loneliness.

Loneliness seems like a simple matter on the surface. The assumption is that if a person is not paired up, or if they have few friends around to keep them company, then they must be lonely. But when loneliness is looked at more closely it isn't as straightforward as that.

Many people who are married with children are still very lonely, while on the other hand, there are many people who live in solitude and are not lonely. Romance doesn't always cure loneliness; it can often exacerbate it (suddenly the person feels insecure when their partner is gone for just a day). And most people tend to feel much lonelier when they are in the wrong company than when they are alone in their own company. Stranger still, if solitude is chosen intentionally, it doesn't carry any sensation of loneliness with it.

So, what is loneliness then, if it's not always cured by close relationships? For sure, it's understandable that people hold this fear. But in many people, it's a little over-the-top. As far as the pursuit of mastery is concerned, usually a person would only need to be able to relax in their own company for a matter of hours without freaking out. It's surprising how rare that ability is, considering that nobody who cares about you now is going to forget about you any time soon. But fortunately, the ability to relax in solitude is one that can be developed through intentional exposure.

[1] Reprinted from *Born for Love: Why Empathy is Essential and Endangered* (William Morrow Paperbacks, 2011) by Bruce Perry

[2] Mihaly Csickszentmihalyi, *Flow: The Psychology of Optimal Experience* (HarperCollins Publishers, 1990), www.harpercollins.com/

[3] Reprinted from *The Lucifer Effect: Understanding How Good People Turn Evil* (Penguin Random House, 2008) by Philip Zimbardo

[4] Reprinted from *Flow: The Psychology of Optimal Experience* (1990) by Mihaly Csikszentmihalyi with permission of HarperCollins Publishers, www.harpercollins.com